GENERATIONS

Generations

Poems by Sam Cornish

Preface by Ruth Whitman

Beacon Press

Copyright © 1968, 1969, 1970, 1971 by Sam Cornish
Library of Congress catalog card number: 70-136227
International Standard Book Number: 0-8070-6414-9
Beacon Press books are published under the auspices of the
    Unitarian Universalist Association
Published simultaneously in Canada by Saunders of Toronto, Ltd.
All rights reserved
Printed in the United States of America

Some of these poems have appeared previously in *Aim, Fire Exit,
Journal of Black Poetry, Massachusetts Review, New American
and Canadian Poetry, American Literary Anthology #3, Poetry
Bag, Red Cedar Review, The Smith,* and *Survival.* Grateful
acknowledgment is made to the editors for permission to reprint.

Photograph in "Others" courtesy of Art Cohen; photograph opposite
title page courtesy of Thomas Edsall; photographs in "Family" and
"Malcolm" courtesy of Julie O'Neil.

This book is for Jean and Carol,
who lived through it.

PREFACE

There have been several periods in American literature since the second World War when it has been fashionable to tout a writer precisely because he is a member of a persecuted minority. The phenomenon is undoubtedly a form of expiation of public guilt for oppression and holocaust. Many Jewish writers directly after the Nazi genocide, and many black novelists and poets, particularly during the past five years, have been the victims of this form of insulting favoritism.

It is sometimes hard during one of these periods to discover whether a Jewish or black writer is trading on the momentary condescension which enables him to publish, or whether he moves in his creative life spontaneously and independently of all current trends. This question can be settled, of course, only by going to the writer's work and witnessing his development over a period of time.

Sam Cornish is not a new poet. He has been writing all his life, first pulling his poems out of a hard unlearned necessity to survive: a poet by instinct, recreating his own experience in new-minted language. Through succeeding years of writing, learning, editing, teaching, he has never lost this original honest and direct access to his subject matter.

But his subject has not only been that of a black boy growing up in Baltimore who sees everything with the intense childlike eye of a poet; or of a young man entering adulthood, marrying, extending his personal and interracial relationships, as all men do.

Of far more importance, his subject is also the tragic history of his race, the human race, the black race. Like the boys in ancient Greece, whose *paideia* was to identify themselves with a Greek hero and try to relive his life, Sam Cornish has the remarkable ability to read himself into other times and people —not as an academic exercise, but as an almost uncanny

transference of personality and sex, as in his poem on
Harriet Tubman:

> . . . I sing to hide
> the sound of my feet;
> dance to conceal
> the pistol under my apron.

He was born with perfect pitch, if you can apply such a
term to a poet's ear. He has an unerring sense of cadence,
of where to break the line. His language—in fact his whole
style—is deceptively simple. It has music, accuracy,
pungency:

> All will die
> watch out for
> the man with the soap
> and the towels

He is a poet who speaks authentically and deeply from his
own human history. His vision goes far beyond the passing
trend; it is, in fact, universal.

Ruth Whitman

CONTENTS

Generations

GENERATIONS 1

he had a name
and no father
packed his books
in milk crates
never reading them just watching
the colors in the afternoon dust

his clothes were patched jersey
he had nothing to say
but watched the strangers
across the street
listened to the fights upstairs

when he was thirteen
he found the yellow seasons of summer
were dark rooms
where girls undressed for boys
he found love in the smooth face of a girl
that has since become darker
and carried more children than he had freckles

he would come into her cold apartment
wondering if he had the special knowledge
that women wanted from men
endured the pain she moaned
the odor between her breasts

and wanted god to remember
he was young

and in much trouble

with himself

Slaves

HOME

home
where my
ground
is

my children
born

my mother's
bone

against the
black

of dirt

the weight
of my father's

box

HARRIET TUBMAN

\# 1

Lord, while I sow earth or song
the sun goes down. My only mother
on a dirt floor is dying, her
mouth open on straw and black
soil, the smell of stew or chicken
in a pot her only memories. I think
of the children
                made in her and sold.

Dry hair falling from her skull,
she moves when my silent feet
come in from the fields. I think
she knows I live her life. What
passes from the mother kills the child
before death.
Lord, you hide behind books
and words.
                   I sing to hide
the sound of my feet;
dance to conceal
the pistol under my apron.

#2 (*from the 1950's*)

harriet tubman you are so
black
you make my mother
cry

go from door to northern
door   black is black your
sin is deeper
than the dust
in your throat

your skin
is a dark place
you live in

my mother twice in her life on worn feet
walked an afternoon against the southern
heat to bring me a ginger cake
her face lined with scars in wrinkled
skin was only twenty three

my mother carried me in the fields and slept
on black ground as i turned within our skin
and as a child white fingers walked into her
mouth to count the teeth and raise the price

i was born somewhere between the shacks
and evenings when shadows were tired across
the fields and dresses gray with dust

JOHN BROWN

john brown
met black
men all his life
his eyes
blue grey
hair growing
low on his forehead
spent his day
behind plow
and bible
walked 12
miles on
meals of potatoes
and cabbage soup

SLAVE MARKET

sleep behind our opened eyes
together in the dark we washed
shaved   practiced grace

arranged by height   color
and sex   we
                    parade

dance in suits
and calico to violin

white men feel teeth   arms
ass

do they understand
the noises
tangled
in the breaking
of families

A DOG LOOKING

a dog looking
for meat
found nat
turner instead

what did
he hear
in the fields
after death

the satisfaction
of murder

SLAVE BURIAL

when
you wear
dead man's
clothing
you die
in a part
of them

bury
the dead
in you
but you
cannot
stop
the death
in fatigues

place
the dead
in the ground
on a hard
board

AGE

age
is for those
with fathers

my mother
lived twelve
miles
distant
she was
my last
place

OTHER NAT TURNERS

george washington
was for the rights
of man
sent his men
to stop his slaves
from sailing
on british ships

phillis wheatly
black in skin
half white in mind
read the bible
went to god and poetry
wrote a poem
for the good general george
kept away from the fields
and slavery
she had a silence
&
another country

his life touched hers
like skin
afraid of itself

MONTGOMERY
(for Rosa Parks)

white woman have you heard
she is too tired to sit in the back
her feet are two hundred years old

move to the back or walk
around to the side door how
long can a woman be a cow

your feet will not move
and you never listen
but even if it rains empty

seats will ride through town
i walk for my children
my feet two hundred years old

Family

sometimes he walked to occupy
his feet

to lower the sky or identify
trees

arrived at home with dust that survived
in his breath

he never fished but counted scattered
boxcars

the death of jungles and natives
in jelly glasses

blew his breath in battered
paper bags

sailed ship for the new world
in the kitchen sink

when asked about his ambition
he always held

his words

THE RIVER

we move from one
land
to another

my sister died
in the river

the cradle
on your sister's
back
is empty

& the water
rises

mother

why do we go
on

if we are
dying

my father carried
a fish over his back
its tail touched the ground

grandmother
used to chain herself
to the postoffice
for women's rights

BROTHER

every year the winter
comes there are so many
of us the house grows warm

brother to brother
skin to skin this
is the way the young sleep

now we have entered
the street   i think
of him he remembers me

my mother lives
through

the burning of
her city

in smoky skin
sleeps

without radio
away from the window

windows fall
through the silent
darkness

in the ruins
my brother carries
a case of beer

his back open to the street

there is not
a sleep deep enough
for her tonight

MY BROTHER IS HOMEMADE

my brother is homemade
like he was the first real
black boy i ever knew

before Richard Wright
or James Baldwin found
black summers
he taught me how to drink at age
five and a half

& cleaned the streets
with bullies and stolen
bread and ice cream

he came into this
color thing lighter
than me
& to prove a point
grew darker
than most

SISTER
(*for Sally*)

1

When she swims,
cold and laughing,
her face unseen,
I stop and listen.
My hands are empty.
I throw greetings
as she comes to keep her promise
with me.
Cocktails and guarded talk.
We drink on the sand
feet in the water. Trees
hide us on the beach.
Not a single word between us
when we talk.

2

she always smiles
her lost feet in small
fur bedroom slippers

arms bend under her breast
she holds herself together
where is the color in her lips

I say her hair so brown
it is talking to me
but she is afraid i am looking

thru her skin

VALERY

you
    wear a blanket
like a movie
                star
    but your feet
    are pointed
    to the floor
when the raft
                is brought to shore
    the trees are bare
                        brother
        carries a dead
eel
    into the house
                    he loves
life
        even while we beat
it with a stick

LOVE POEM

my head
            caving
        in
have
            you ever been
loved like
            this?

APRIL 68

somewhere cities burn
my wife is sleeping
i touch her face
and find the cheeks
are wet
there is something
being said

Barns grow slowly out of the dark
Rain disappears in the night
Birds are building nests in dry and private places
Your tongue spits and clicks in sleep.

Some of us in laundromats eating
cold hamburgers watching the lonely small town roads
are covered with hundreds of years
and western skin.

One by one trees touch us.
I hear grass breaking in rabbits' teeth.

WIFE

in the dark
trying to be
alone a woman
must be a wife

a man must work
to earn his hour
& thinks a woman's
day is filled

with extra hours
blind to her
he steals her sleep
and reads the paper

YOUR MOTHER

your mother
in the market
place searches
for fish
pinches oranges
watches prices
change for
the weekend
she checks the dirt
under the butcher's
fingernail her feet
slip in water
and fish scales
hamburger looks
dead behind dirty
counter glass
flies
even in the winter
live here

SOONER OR LATER

sooner or later
somebody dies
in your family
& you got to know
what to do
or you are going
to feel bad
when the women
pull out
their hankerchiefs
& your hands
are still
in your pockets

WINTERS

When I start to think of myself as a child, I always begin with winters. Do any of you remember how you learned the taste of warm milk, the smell of oil on your fingers, or the look of steps covered with ice, the first time. No. This is calendar work. All that keeps with me is the silences of my childhood winters when the absence of my father kept me close to the first two women in my life. Being alone with them, my brother and I were close for two boys, and they grew the same way. It was like the four of us in the world, living through meal time and seasons.

We lived through the dying smells of September without knowing it was the end of summer my brother and me, long trips through streets already black with cloud, our feet loud in those empty streets of windowed shuttered houses, looking for newspapers, or smoke from passing trains. If we encountered people, I don't remember it now. It was like everything being reduced to leaves and small streets where packages of newspapers sit on the curbs.

It was the most natural thing being without a father. You just never saw him in the house. Suddenly you were in the world. No memories except you were moving around doing things. This is how it begins. It's like you were always there, and he never was.

I suppose there is a sadness to this: images of women alone in their rooms unable to drink or dance life into their long and vacant lives without husbands or relations, winters so cold the toilet freezes under you, and most of all the rats that squeak in the night, the mice that walk through the kitchen looking for food, as you must have looked for food, and candies. But you lived and while you are alive there is the joy of living, this is what keeps.

I think this is what I want to write about: the life behind the broken faces or finished hands. Something goes on, even death picks the life out of your legs. I have seen it. The streets where men dig in the dust of their pockets to fool themselves. A man unable to kill because we are brothers and his knife is at your throat, and must be at his also. Hunger so deep your eyes cannot attend to the things before them. Winters so cold that the fingers break off and the hand hangs there.

But through it all we live, and it is all we will ever know.

My mother always said that we would grow up and leave her. She spent so much time saying this that my grandmother began to repeat her remark while scrubbing my back. This is the reason why to this day my back is lighter than my chest.

My grandmother was a yellow woman looking more like a visiting white lady from the big house than one of us, and at that time she almost acted like it. She was big on manners, and hard on those who picked their nose, didn't wipe after leaving the toilet; most of all she was saying that the devil would get you if you fucked around too much.

Being raised by two women who thought they were going to be left behind when the men in the family grew up, growing among two aging women who regretted their marriages was the background that made and separated my brother and me. When I want to remember him, it is always a matter of starting with the words or images of the women who, after our father's death, raised us. These women raised us on two things: chicken and God.

I knew little of the world outside, but sensed a kind of beauty in the streets that threw leaves and shadows so carefully through our house. We went to school, church, and to the house of our only relationship without being aware of the people in the street being rich, poor, middle class, or white. The only recollection we have of poverty was the day we came home and there was nothing to eat for lunch, and my grandmother made gravy from flour and water. We went back to school ready to read our books with a warm and friendly belly. This was the way I remembered it. I'm certain this was the way it was.

But this is the common work of memory. Now when I want to know myself, there is nothing for me to work with.

I start with pictures.

The street was always outside of the house. It never went anywhere except under the snow. There it rested with a deeper silence than sleep. Men emerged out of the weather with red faces concealed by ice and woolen scarves. The feet itched in the boots until the snow went away. But this is a slow thing, of silence emerging black under the ice, or the crust of the snow broken by foot and shovel. The street was there after all. But it seemed to go away for a while.

During this time of the year we were cold. All of the doors of the house remained shut, and we slept four in a bed. The single light in the house: oil lamp light after dark with the shades drawn, going over the rim, the dim flame glows behind the globe. All day she rubs the globe with newspapers and at night this clears the lamp for lighting. Outside there is the whiteness of snow and silence. I don't remember if we ate much during our winters; there was one Christmas tree that died in our house, and one turkey dinner. But winter means white curtains, the early lighting of the lamp. Up and down the streets the lights go on and off, the street car rings its bell till morning. We sleep.

I feel I have lived my life in winters. I feel my life has been the life of four people in a house surrounded by the silences of snow, the coming and going of lights in my neighbor's house. I know people lived on my street, but I never knew the color of their skin. We lived alone and in each other. Snow turns my fingers red. Snow is the color of my grandmother's dying hair. The images of winter are the ice in her dead eyes. Ice is how my growing mother slips on the winter ground. Cold is the house we live in. Our bodies the places where we stay and are warm in our home. But I ask myself if we always lived in Febrary or December how come we were never able to speak the word love. Too busy with the blood that stands up in the skin in winter to speak of things, we can only go on living.

My mother always said we would go on without her. What else was there for us to do. Nobody stayed in these old houses; in the dark silence of those places you could only die. There my father died and my grandmother slowly rotted. Across the alley from our first home my mother sits today waiting to die. She picks among her life for things to do, as you and I, but I think she waits. Now she is older. Her children gone.

There should be no pity for her. I see in the eyes of my friends a concern, because she is a woman in an old house. Her children thinking of children of their own, a home to finish their lives in; what is there for her to do but sit out the seasons in dated clothing. But I have seen her drinking at my wedding or shaking her head when dandruff falls on my shoulders; I saw her laughing with two teeth going brown in her mouth, and I felt her lips struggle on my face because after thirty-one years, her sons are learning the gestures of loving. In her small rooms in silence she sits, and she lives.

42

Malcolm

MALCOLM

Malcolm, I think of you when I read
the papers of the SWP
and hear the boys on winter street
corners selling the newspapers late
into the night, the next day, the day after
and the following weekend

Malcolm, I think of you when I wash
my hair and look at a can of grease,
or young punks seeking old men
with ice picks and broken bottles,
wanting nickles for wine.

Malcolm, I think of you when I remember
the death of JFK and black children
who for no reason wet their eyes.

Malcolm, I think of you when I walk home
after leaving a street of poor white and
hear you are dead and see all the white
faces behind their own prisons and windows.

I think of you now and know
this day has become many years.

EMPTY DOORWAYS

Empty doorways come straight
at me

Faces growing in the windows,
quiet women hanging clothes in the backyard,

indians are falling in the streets.
I hear Malcolm X is dead;

they become white.

FOR THE MOTHER OF MALCOLM X

a yellow woman she knew
her words and used them well

watching white men on horseback
her child heavy between
her legs

she thought she saw her father
he could have been

a man bringing a cross
into her yard that night

ONE EYED BLACK MAN IN NEBRASKA

The skin quickens to noises.
The ground beneath a black man opens.

His wife in her nightgown
hears horses and men in her husband's
deathbed

white horses move through the fields
lifting men out of the darkness.

In the pillows she kept
a rifle and twenty two,
for hunting rabbits and keeping alive.

Still he died,
his one eye closed on the ground.

REMEMBERED

if Malcolm X read a book
or called me brother
if Malcolm X wanted to be a laborer
but went to jail instead

he measured his world
and made it black

now the summer crumbles into fall
and the CIA recruits on black campuses
white housewives take target practice

the white man buys his ground
and moves his children, his taxes,
while black women crowd their families
into their bodies and small apartments
growing smaller each year

and men are eager to die
from boredom
from hunger
from women who feel hands under their clothes
in integrated parking lots   welfare checks
that work only for drugs and back rent   jobs
that quit before a man is employed

if Malcolm X measured his world
white men with family
and god   track us down
with cinderblocks

YOU CAN BURN A CITY WITH A RENT BOOK

stuff a house
until it is dark with people

hang a man by his wrist
and make him black

nail a man to the ground
pour food into his mouth
salt and pepper his eyes

something is under his skin
look at each other
his skin is as dark as mine

LOW INCOME HOUSING

there is a cop on the corner
he wants a five pound bag of sugar
for Christmas

at the window we move
dark shadows on the street
in the house we get out of long beds
and touch the cold

at the windows your eyes are ruined
there is a cop on the corner

women with lunch bags enter the streetcar
their eyes pop
in each heavy mouth the same dark space
between the gums

there is a cop on the corner
he breaks your teeth when he comes into the house
he says the jew is counting money

#1

housing projects
above the rooftops
stop the colors
of the sky
erase street corners
send my neighbors
to hide behind white
and angry talk

black skin
at the windows   faces
laughing throughout
the word day   radios
that sing
in teenagers' hands
the mindless songs
of those with flat feet
and boys' names

the old should be left alone

                              fixed with memories
                              of plantations never owned
                              atlanta bus stations
                              with two waiting rooms
                              brothers who worked
                              twenty years
                              stuffing mail bags
                              making telephone wire

but the city fathers
throw the streets
away   old people mourn
the front yards left
alone to die

repeat
in me
repeat again the places
the history
            of people kept
            to themselves ugly
            and unwilling to work
            who push their lives
            against us

#2

the greyhound bus
the low income high rise
the purse snatchers
who die from wounds in the back of the head
            soap in prison showers
the passengers who smoke
cigars or spit
on the floors of the house
next door
are killing grandparents
of the college girl
and she kisses the flag
waves the flag
in the face of the poor
and all the poor she sees
are black

her grandmother's eyes go round
and dark like the wheels
of the greyhound her eyes dim
with smoke   the windows
break every afternoon
when at four thirty

the traffic is so long
passing in front of her
house she has to wash
all the clothes she hung
up to dry in the afternoon

from the highrise children
drop bicycle wheels   learn
to steal grass out
of her front yard   adults
watch her from shopping carts
filled with welfare food
her dresses grow longer
children run through
her yard laughing
at an old woman's legs

and taxes for education
buy drinks in negro bars
laws are passed so white children
cannot go to school

and all the world she watches is black
the smoke of the factories working her husband
the bicycle wheels dropped from windows
the fumes of evening traffic   coming together
the nights that have lost their silence
all the faces behind shopping carts

CROSSING OVER INTO DELAWARE
DURING THE NEWARK RIOTS

traffic stops
on the bridges
rivers twist
steamships
oil changes
the colors
of southern
beaches

at the docks
& waterways
of northern
cities
longshoremen
watch the water
cargo six months
old in
maryland ships

on the streets
headlines rolled
into fist

between the river
city and bridge
a darkness
in the air
the wind is spreading

Others

DORY MILLER

(black man who earned
a purple heart at Pearl Harbor)

he left the kitchen
long enough to earn a purple
heart

downed three planes before
the death
of his ship

when he died
four yellow dead men
on his hands

he was still peeling potatoes
his medal somewhere in the pages
of a book

NEIGHBORS

There was an old man
with a woodstove and dirty underwear,
a wife who ran away.
We went to his house,
called him pop.
Chopped his wood, defended his cookies
from rats, roaches,
enforced his needle with thread.
Spread cold water over his coal covered
dusty floor.
Spoke to pictures of his dead
children.
Admired the dirt on his bed, searched
his comb for dandruff and hair.
He went away somewhere
to die.

PANTHER

(Bobby Hutton, murdered by the Oakland police)

three black boys
listen to the sounds
around them

in the trees policemen
are growing sticks

there are 20 holes
in bobby
his life runs through
them

DEATH OF DR. KING

#1

we sit outside
the bars   the dime stores
everything is closed today

we are mourning
our hands filled with bricks
a brother is dead

my eyes are white and cold
water is in my hands

this is grief

2

after the water
the broken bread
we return
to our separate
places

in our heads
bodies collapse
and grow again

the city boils
black men
jump out of trees

RAY CHARLES

do you
dig ray
charles

when the
blues are
silent

in his throat

& he rolls
up his
sleeves

MEMO

robert kennedy the next morning
look around and see all the boyhood
growing under tenements
finding all the ways of mixing
sand and gasoline
look around and see the children
do not understand these buildings
are too old for you
to die in

NEWSCAST
(*1968 Republican Convention*)

four dead
in florida
the long night
is ending

the national guard
is cleaning chicken
and pork chops
off the street

the looters
were running
with seeds
spilling
from their lips

CHILDREN AFTER SCHOOL

woolen coats
held together
by pin
        or button
come into
the afternoon
                beating
black board
erasers

dust on four
hands
        in watery
eyes

happy with
the afternoon
        legs
dancing
    under coats
making the
        noises
of children
out of school
    but in love   with teach

BLACK CHILD

if jesus
            eyes
are blue
            I
stay
      with my
  doll

GOOD FRIDAY AND SUNDAY MORNING

good friday and sunday morning
through the countryside and small town

we listen to the radio
songs sex memories of dr king

the mayor eats a cold nervous
& late supper on the freeway

the son of stepen fechitt oils
his rifle the national guards

cancel leave the mayor kneels
before the ghettoes

the only sounds college boys
going to new england

american flag decals
on their windows

WALKS

the coldness inside
of the overcoats
of newsboys
encounters the evening

every man a coated
place away from
home   his skin
bruised by newspapers

going home church
bells ring inside
of me

the grocer
is counting change
behind a locked door

POVERTY WORKER
(*for the Enoch Pratt Library*)

Lord,
    when I think
of your hands
        my milk
shake
    gets warm,
        and I
want to stay
        with the poor
and go into their
          shacks.

When I see your crown,
and know you have suffered
for us,
    I sit on these dark
chairs.
      The smoke of coal
fires and bodies
        are those
of your world
      also,
        these
are your dark people.
            I want
to help them lord,
        with prayer
patience,
    and night school
classes,
    and maybe someday
they be middle class
and drink of your blood,
and eat
    of your body.

BIGGER THOMAS SAYS SOME BAD
NIGGERS IS OVER THIRTY

Bigger Thomas with a pillow as a weapon
mean enough to turn feathers
into cinderblocks (and that's something
even jesus can't do)

Bigger Thomas in Cleveland
breaking the heart of Carl Stokes
looking for Malcolm
for Stokely
for Rap

Bigger Thomas in Watts
in Detroit
out of work and his mother, his friends,
all the girls on the block,
saying he's lazy

Bigger Thomas cutting up the pool table
pissing in the collection plate
what is that boy worth?
there goes a brick through the
pawnshop window

Bigger
where did you get all those tv sets
(in color too)
Bigger Thomas
scaring his sister
working a rat between his teeth

Bigger Thomas on the roof cleaning
a rifle

"What kind of progress is this?"
asks Edward Brooke

Bigger Thomas
your head is black and just think
you were born sometime around nineteen thirty-nine

A BLACK MAN

a black man
in the water
stands
in sand and cold
stones
push on his feet
like any other man

did I expect something
different
because
we are another kind
of man

the first
and last
the one who the convoy
comes for
the new man in the ovens

Afterword

FORECAST

All will die
watch out for
the man with the soap
and the towels

Born in 1935, Sam Cornish has lived in
Baltimore most of his life. He has spent time
in the United States army and with an insurance
company, and, from 1966 to 1970 was a writing
specialist with the Neighborhood Centers in
Baltimore. He is currently a special teacher
in creative writing at the Highland Schools
in Roxbury, Massachusetts. He is the co-editor
of *Chicory,* an anthology of poems and writings
from the black ghetto, and the co-author of
Your Hand in Mine, a children's book. His own
poetry has been anthologized by Clarence Major
and Leroi Jones, among others, and has appeared
in such magazines as *Journal of Black Poetry,*
Massachusetts Review, and *The Smith.*